Rhythmic Relevance

Rhythmic Relevance

Andre Townsend

The TNT Group

Contents

1

∾

<u>Rhythmic Relevance</u>
Poetry Collection
Andre Townsend
Preface

Rhythmic Relevance is a poetry book that delves into the complexities and contradictions of modern life. Written by poet and author Andre Townsend, the collection explores a wide range of themes, including love, loss, identity, and the human condition.

Throughout the book, Andre writes about the small moments that often go unnoticed in our busy lives, but that hold great significance. He writes about the joys and sorrows of daily life, the beauty of nature, and the struggles of the human spirit. The poems are both personal and universal, and her use of imagery and metaphor helps to bring her message to life.

One of the recurring themes in the book is the idea of epiphany or the realization of something profound and meaningful. Andre's poems often capture these moments of insight, whether they are small revelations or life-changing epiphanies. Lamenting on the power of these moments to change us, to open our eyes to the world around us, and to bring us closer to understanding ourselves and our place in the world.

Throughout the collection, the writing is both powerful and evocative, as his words have a way of reaching into the soul and stirring emotions, coupled with his unique ability to convey the simple truths of everyday life in a way that is both profound and relatable.

Table of Contents

My perfect IMPERFECTION	41		Talk that talk	42
Mikan under the kotatsu	43		Thought to myself	44
Model Role	45		Ramble	46
How I feel vs. How I look	47		Temper Temper	48
Forces	49		Realize	50

• **Yesterday**

Yesterday, a memory now A glimpse of the past, a fading vow Once full of life, now just a shadow Of all that once was, we must let go
The laughter and the tears, all gone by The people and the places, no longer nigh But in our hearts, they will always stay As we remember yesterday
The joy and the pain, the love, and the strife All part of the journey, the dance of life But yesterday is gone, and today is here And we must make the most of it, dear
So let us not dwell on what's been done But look ahead to what is yet to come For every day is a chance to start anew And yesterday, though gone, will always be a part of you.
Don't rush the brush and waste the paint, Scribble

Scribble, page today, Tomorrow is new, Manifest positive to come
true
Rainy yesterday, clear skies today, Another chance to roll the die
Yesterday was yesterday
Yesterday is gone, forever in the past, Memories of laughter, memories of pain
Moments of joy and moments that didn't last, All now just memories, some clear, some faint.
Yesterday's struggles, we all have faced, Challenges we overcame, lessons we've learned
Yesterday's triumphs, we all have graced, Victories we've won, bridges we've burned.
Yesterday's love, we all have known, Heartache and happiness, passion and pain
Yesterday's friendships, we all have shown, Loyalties tested, bonds that remain.
Yesterday is gone, but its story lives on, In the choices we make, the paths we choose
Yesterday's memories, and in our hearts they're drawn,
As we look ahead, to a brighter tomorrow, to renew.

• **Comparison**

Comparison, the thief of joy, Steals the beauty of today,
Making us focus on what's not, Instead of what we've got.
It whispers in our ears at night, That we're not good enough, not
right,

It tells us we should be like them, But who are they, and where does it end?
We look at others with envious eyes, Wishing for their perfect lives,
But we forget that life is not a game, And we all have our own unique flame.
So let us put down this heavy load, Of constant comparison, and let it go,
For life is short, and time is fleeting, Let's embrace our own unique being

• Brand New Toy

New pleasure, sweet and pure, Like a ray of sunlight on a meadow. It fills my heart and warms my soul, And I am forever grateful to know.
It comes in many forms, A new friend, a lover's kiss, A song that speaks to me, Or simply a moment of bliss.
It's the small things that count, A smile from a stranger, A kind word from a friend, That make life worth the danger.
So let us all embrace, The new pleasure life brings, For it is a precious gift, That happiness brings
Brand new toys, shiny and bright, In boxes and bags, they take flight. With colors so bold and designs so grand, These toys will make anyone's heart expand.
Their buttons and gears, a wonder to see, With endless possibilities, they set the imagination free. They come in all shapes, sizes and hues, no matter their muse.
From dolls and cars, to brand purses and blocks, Brand new toys,

always in demand, never in stocks. So let us play, and let minds grow,
With brand new toys, dreams will always flow.

• **Fall down, get up**

When all seemed lost and hope was scarce, And doubts and fears had risen to par, I found the strength to rise above, And faced the impossible with a heart of love.

I knew that I had nothing to lose, But everything to gain, So I pushed through the pain, And found the strength to rise again.

With every step I took, I felt my confidence grow, And soon I knew I had to go, And face the impossible head-on, with a heart aglow.

I reached deep down inside And found the courage to fight, And though the odds were stacked against me, I knew that I had to try with all my might.

I battled through the storm, And emerged victorious in the end, For I had overcome the impossible, And found the strength to rise again.

Though life may be a struggle, And the path ahead may seem unclear, Just remember to keep on fighting, And you'll overcome the impossible, my dear.

Rising from the ashes, A phoenix reborn. A comeback so fierce, A story untold.

Once defeated and broken, Left for dead and alone. But a spark still remained, A fire yet unblown.

With determination in heart, And grit in every step. The comeback began, With a will to reprep.

Through trials and tribulations, With each fall, grew stronger. The comeback was made, A victory longer.
Now standing tall, With head held high. A comeback complete, A new chapter to write.
For in every defeat, Lies the seed of a win. And with time, effort, Comebacks always begin

• **Opportunity**

Opportunity knocks, but once, they say
A chance to seize, or let slip away To take it up, or let it be A decision made, for eternity
It's easy to miss, in the flow of days A moment gone, in so many ways A missed connection, a closed door A regret that lingers evermore
But when we do, when we take the leap When we seize the chance and make it ours to keep The world opens wide, and all is new A path unfolds, that we never knew
So take the opportunity, when it arises For you'll never know, what it truly prizes A chance to live, to love, to learn A chance to grow, and make a turn
Opportunity knocks, but once, they say A chance to seize, or let slip away The choice is yours, to make or miss The chance to live, a life of bliss.

• **Competition**

Competition sharpens the blade
Rivals fuel the fire within Each push and shove, a test of strength To
rise above and win
The thrill of the race, the heat of the fight Pushing past what we
thought we could bear For in the end, it's not about the prize But the
journey and the growth we share
With every obstacle and every foe We learn to dig deep and strive To
become the best version of ourselves And to truly come alive
So let the competition rage on For it is in the challenge we thrive For
every rival we face Brings us one step closer to being alive.

• **MASK**

A mask upon my face, A symbol of this trying time, A shield against
the unseen grace, A reminder that we all must climb.

The climb to health and safety, The climb to peace and ease, The climb to end this disparity, The climb to bring the world to its knees.

But even as we wear these masks, And do our part to keep the peace, Let us not forget the tasks, That still lie ahead with a never-ending lease.

Let us not forget the fight, The fight for freedom and for choice, For though we wear these masks at night, We still must raise our voices.

So let us wear our masks with pride, A symbol of our strength and will, For though the climb may be long and hard, Together, we will conquer still.

• **Foreign**

In a foreign land, new sights to see Culture and customs, so different from me Excitement and wonder, fill my heart As I journey to a brand new start

Through winding streets, and crowded bazaars I take in the sights, and breathe in the air The spicy scent of food, so unique A taste sensation, my taste buds seek

The people I meet, so kind and warm Their language may be different, but their love is the norm Their stories and traditions, so rich and deep I am grateful for the chance to learn and keep

But as my trip comes to an end I know I'll be back, to see my new friends For the memories I've made, will stay with me Of my travels in a foreign country.

Traveling is a journey of the mind, A trip through time, a way to unwind.

From mountains high to oceans wide, The world is yours to explore and abide.

With every step, a new story unfolds, As you break free from the familiar mold.

The sights and sounds, the people you meet, Will leave you feeling alive, complete.

So pack your bags and set out on your way, For traveling is the ultimate play.

Go out and explore, learn and grow, For the world is waiting, don't let it go.

Embrace the unknown, take a chance, For the memories you make will be worth the dance.

• **Manchild**

Childish men, with minds so small, Acting out, like they're in a hall. Throwing fits, with no regard, For the words they speak, or the cards they've dealt.

They stomp their feet, and pound their chest, As if to say, "I am the best!" But their actions speak a different tale, One of immaturity, and a lack of scale.

They can't see past their own desires, Their wants and needs, set on fire. They lash out, with little thought, And leave behind, those they've fought.

But they'll learn, in time, to grow, And leave their childhood, far below. They'll learn to think, before they act, And their childish ways, they'll retract.

Until then, we'll shake our heads, At the men who are still in beds.
Unable to see, what they lack, And the true meaning of being a man.
Men are boys, forever young With minds that race and hearts that
run They play and fight and make some noise Their innocence, forever
joys
They chase their dreams and dare to soar Their spirits free, forever
more They laugh and love and live with fire Their souls ablaze, their
hearts a choir
But as they grow and years go by They learn the weight of the world's
sighs And though they may feel lost at times They always find the
strength to climb
For men are boys, forever strong Their hearts and minds forever long
For adventure and for growth, they strive Their boyish souls, forever
alive

• **Self-Esteem**

Self-esteem, a treasure to hold
Deep within, it makes us bold It gives us strength to face each day
And chase our fears away
It's not about being perfect But about being true To who we are and
what we do Self-esteem helps us to see The beauty in our own unique
key
It helps us to stand tall And not let others make us fall It gives us the
courage to be Our authentic selves, truly free
So let us nurture and treasure Our self-esteem with pleasure For it is
the foundation Of a life filled with elation

Self-esteem, a treasure so dear, A feeling that's hard to come by, But when it's found, it's crystal clear, It makes life worth living, and fly.
It's not about being perfect, Or having all the right things, It's about accepting your own worth, And spreading your wings.
With self-esteem, you'll find, That you can conquer fear, And reach for the stars, And make your dreams appear.
So hold your head up high, And be proud of who you are, For you are unique and special, And your self-esteem will take you far.

• **Rabbit Hole**

Distractions all around, Never a moment to be found, Thoughts scattered in the breeze, A constant hum of mental unease.
The phone dings, the email pings, A million tasks on endless strings, A pull to check, to scroll, to see, A cycle hard to break, to be free.
The mind wanders, the heart races, An endless stream of thoughts and faces, A constant chatter, a never-ending noise, A distracting joy, and distracting poise.
But in the stillness, in the quiet, A chance to clear, to focus, to try it, To let go of the distractions and the noise, And find a moment of inner joys.
So let us strive to find peace, Away from distractions, a moment of release, For in the stillness, we will find, A clearer mind, a happier mind.

• The Giver

Giving with open hands,
A heart full of love, A spirit free from demands, From the heavens above.
The joy that it brings, To both you and me, A dance on the wings, Of generosity.
A simple act, yet so grand, It echoes through time, A gesture that can change a man, And make his heart shine.
So let us give, with all our might, With every breath we take, For in giving, we find delight, And our souls truly awake.
For giving is not just about the gift, But the love that it brings, A heart full of grace and lift, And the joy that it sings.
Give with an open heart, And a smile on your face, For the joy that you'll impart, Will bring a special grace.
Give without expectation, For that is true giving, And the love and adoration, Will be yours for the living.
Give of your time and your treasure, Give of your love and your care, For in giving we find the greatest pleasure, And a life that is truly rare.
So give with all of your might, For in giving we truly live, For the love that we ignite, Will forever give and give

• **Vanity**

Vanity, oh vanity,
A curse upon the mind, A never-ending cycle, Of seeking to be kind.
We preen and we primp, We pose and we prance, All in the pursuit,
Of a fleeting glance.
But what do we gain, From all of our toil, A momentary ego boost, A
shallow, fleeting foil.
For true beauty lies, Not in the mirror's glass, But in the kindness of
our hearts, And the love that will last.
So let us cast aside, This vanity so vain, And seek true beauty, That
will forever remain.

• **Family**

Family ties that bind us tight, Sometimes lead to bitter fights.

Words said in anger, hearts filled with pride, Leaving wounds that
won't easily subside.
But despite the disagreements and all the hurtful words we've spoken,
We must remember one thing true, our family bond is unbroken.
For though we may not see eye to eye, and our tempers may rise and
fall,
In the end, it's family that holds us high,
Through it all, through it all.
So let us strive to understand, and to forgive and to forget,
For in the end, it's love that makes a family, a bond we'll never regret.

• **Cheaters never Prosper**

Cheaters may win in the short term, But in the long run, they will
lose. Their lies and deceit will catch up, And their actions will them
bruise.
They may gain temporary pleasure, But soon their guilt will gnaw.
Their conscience will not let them rest, And their relationships will fall.
They will lose the trust of others, And their reputation will be
tarnished. Their reputation is hard to earn But easy to be banished.
Honesty and integrity, Are the keys to success. Cheating may bring
short-lived gains, But it will lead to nothingness.

So if you're tempted to cheat, Think twice before you do. For in the long run, cheaters lose, And the truth will always come through.

• **Trust**

Learning is the key to unlock the door, To a world of knowledge, forevermore.
It opens up our minds and sets us free, To explore and discover, to be, to see.
It helps us understand the world around, And to find our place, and make our own ground.
It teaches us to think and to create, To imagine and to innovate.
It gives us the power to adapt and grow, To face the challenges that life bestow.
So let us learn and learn again, For it is the seed that will forever sustain.
The tree of knowledge will forever stand, A beacon of light in this great land.
So let us learn and learn with pride, For it is the key to the future we abide.

• **Forgotten**

In alleys dark and corners low, Lives a people few of us know. Their
struggles and their pain, Are things we'd rather not sustain.
They've fallen on hard times, And the world has committed crimes.
Against these souls forgotten, Their struggles we have not noticed.
But in their eyes, there's a light, That shines so bright and bold, And
in their hearts, there's a fire, That burns with stories untold.
Their lives may be low, But they're fighters, don't you know? They'll
rise above their station, With determination and patience.
So let us not forget, These low life people yet, For in their struggles,
we'll find, A strength that's pure and kind

- **Mental Slavery**

Trapped in a cage of my own mind, I struggle to break free from the
binds. Thoughts that control and thoughts that confine, A prison that's
hard to leave behind.
The shackles of doubt and fear, Hold me captive year after year. I try
to escape but it's not clear, How to break the chains that hold me here.
My mind is a slave to negative thought, It's a cycle that's hard to be
caught. I want to break free but it's so fraught, With fear and uncertainty
that it's all for naught.
But I will not give up the fight, I'll keep pushing through the night.
I'll find a way to make things right, And escape the mental slavery that
holds me tight.
For I am more than my mind, I am strong, and I am kind. I will not
let it control me, I'll break free and live my life wild and free.

idea   planning   strategy   success

• **Success**

Success is a journey, not a destination, A path that we all must tread, With each step we take, we learn and grow, And gain the strength to go ahead.

It's found in the moments of triumph, When we've reached a long-sought goal, But also in the times of struggle, When we've had to dig deep and roll.

It's not about the fame and glory, Or the riches that we acquire, But about the person that we become, And the fire that burns within our fire.

So if you're searching for success, Don't look too far or too wide, For it's within yourself you'll find it, And the journey is the prize.

Success is not a destination, But a journey on the way, With each step we take, We learn and grow each day.

We strive for greatness, And push ourselves to the limit, For success is not given, But earned through hard work and grit.

We face obstacles, And sometimes fall, But we must rise again, And stand tall.

For success is not final, And failure is not fatal, We must keep moving forward, And never settle for mediocre.

So let us chase our dreams, And never give up the fight, For true success, Lies just within our sight.

• **Seasons**

Seasons come and seasons go, Nature's cycles ever flow. Winter brings the snow and cold, But also tales to be told.
Spring brings new life to the land, Birds return, with a song in hand. Flowers bloom, the sun shines bright, Nature awakens after a long night.
Summer brings warmth and light, Days are long, everything is bright. Birds sing, children play, Nature is alive in every way.
Autumn brings the falling leaves, Colors change, nature grieves. But it's a time of preparation, For the next cycle of creation.
Seasons come and seasons go, Nature's cycles ebb and flow. Each one unique, each one new, Nature's beauty forever true.
The seasons change with graceful ease, Each one a work of art, With colors bright, and winds that tease, They make a brand new start.
In spring, the flowers bloom anew, And all the world awakens, The grass is green, the sky is blue, And nature's heart is shaken.
In summer, days are long and hot, The sun shines bright and strong, The fields are green, the bees are not and the nature's song
In fall, the leaves are turning red, And gold, and orange, and brown, The air is crisp, the days are short, And autumn wears a crown.
In winter, snowflakes softly fall, And cover all the ground, The trees are bare, the days are short, But still a beauty found.
So let us cherish every season, Each one a work of art, For nature's beauty has no reason, It simply is, and that's a start.

• **Love**

Love will get you altered worse than any drug will, Heart at a stand-
still
True love is a feeling pure and true, A bond that forever will renew,
It's not just a fleeting glance or a kiss, But a love that forever will persist.
It's a love that is selfless and kind, That leaves you feeling warm inside, It's a love that is patient and true, And will see you through anything you'll do.
True love is a treasure to behold, A love that forever will be told, It's a
love that will never grow old, And a love that will always be bold.
So hold on tight to true love's hand, And cherish it throughout all of
life's lands, For true love is worth all the fight, And will be your guiding
light

• **Solace**

In moments of despair and woe, A solace can be hard to know. But if you look deep within your heart, You'll find a spark that will not depart. Though the road ahead may be long and steep, With every step, you'll start to reap,

The rewards of your perseverance, And find a sense of inner reverence.

For in the darkest of the night, A glimmer of hope shines bright. And though the storm may rage and roar, It's in the quiet that we find solace once more.

So when the world around you seems so cold, Remember that you are not alone. For there is a light that guides the way, And in its warmth, you'll find solace today.

All around, no need to look, Introvert, extrovert

Protect my worth, protect my hurt,

Peace in the silence, Noise in my head

Inner peace minus the conforms of society, Be selfish to yourself, solace

In moments of despair, When all hope seems lost,

Solace can be found, In the beauty of the frost.

With each flake that falls, A reminder that though life is fleeting, Its beauty is eternal, And peace is always within our reaching.

So let us find solace, In the simple things,

The warmth of a smile, The joy that love brings.

For though the storms may rage, And the winds may howl,

In the stillness of the heart, Solace can be found.

So take a deep breath, And let the worries fade,

For in the stillness of the soul, Peace can be made.

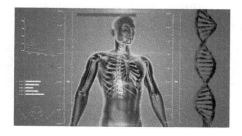

• X-Ray

Thoughts swirl like a tempest inside, A mystery to the casual observer. But those who read minds see inside, To the secrets that others try to cover.

Like pages in a book unread, The mind holds tales yet to unfold. But those who read minds see ahead, And know the story yet to be told.

With every thought and every feeling, They decipher what lies beneath. And in the mind's depths, they're revealing The truth that others cannot see.

But with great power comes great responsibility, And those who read minds must be true. For with the gift of insight, they'll see The beauty and the darkness too.

So let us read minds with care, And use our gift to help, not harm. For the thoughts of others are precious and rare, And should be treated with reverence and charm

I can see under your smile, If it's a smile

Mirrors a child, hard to disguise. I see under, I smile too, in case you wonder

Am I too, hypocritical to keep the peace

Still, waters run deep, tongue in cheek

Mind's ocean deep, I can see under that nervous grin

Nervous laugh, if I cared I would take you to task

Wear that mask, we both deserve an Oscar

Well that is if you think I am agreeable, the one holding the blade unforeseeable

under your complimentary nature, Your eyes throw off the courtesy

Are you a hater? Your body language is not in sync

Subtle as it may be, like an X-ray, I can see

• **Friend**

True friendship is a treasure rare, A bond that's strong and always there. Through laughter and through tears we share, In joy and sorrow, always a pair.

With open hearts and open minds, We walk together, step by step, With trust and love that's hard to find, Our friendship is a bond that's kept.

No distance or time can break the tie, That binds our hearts in unity, Through every challenge, we rely, On each other's company.

A listening ear, a helping hand, A shoulder to cry on, a friend to stand, With true friendship, life is grand, A love that never comes to an end.

Faithful thy friend who's more valuable than anything monetary

A bird in hand is worth two in the bush can or can't be true

An old friend is more valuable than possessing three that's new,

A friend can we say you are one?

No one is perfect, but as long as we are strong in our deeds

A friend indeed, Grip my heart, with your touch

- **Elated**

Happy thoughts fill my mind As I walk through fields of gold The
sun shines bright and warm And my heart feels bold
I breathe in the fresh air And feel my spirits lift I'm so grateful for this
moment And all the joy it brings
I dance with the butterflies And sing with the birds I soak in the
beauty Of all the world has to offer
Life is a precious gift And I'm so happy to be alive I'll cherish every
moment And never take it for granted
So let us all be happy And spread love and light For in this world of
ours Happiness is what makes everything right
Got up feeling like I can move mountains,
burned my breakfast however it still tasted good, took a longer
shower than usual,
running late but I am not running or driving fast, enjoying the
moment making it last
focused on the positives kept my mood on a keel
birthday acknowledged belated, there is no rain on my parade, I am
elated

• **Virgins do it better**

Virgins pure and untainted, Innocence in their eyes, A beauty that's unacquainted With the world's deceitful lies.
Their hearts are like a rosebud, Closed tight, yet full of grace, A treasure yet to be understood, A future yet to take its place.
They walk with heads held high, Their steps unmarred by fear, Their souls untouched by sighs, Their hearts without a tear.
Their laughter is like music, Their words a sweet refrain, A symphony of magic, That can ease away all pain.
So let us honor virgins, For their purity and light, May they always be given The respect they deserve, and right
Patience is measured by the time one spends being chased, healing of one's broken heart needs a virgin, one must know a virgin's inner personality is equatable to a dark cave,
One encounter whether premeditated or spontaneous can leave one's virginity,Turn that omelet into an egg, irreversible when broken, Virgin was once, Virgin was valued, virgin got me open, Entry needle eyed, Waterfall when I got inside

,

• Hunimals

How are animal taken care of? Open the cages, Are we animals?
Want to see how a bird flies, We are the most dangerous creature
Pollution, global warming, hunting, fishing species to extinction

Humans may have evolved to walk on two legs and create civ-
ilizations, but at the core of our being, we are still animals driven
by instinct and survival.

We may have the ability to reason and think abstractly, but
that does not make us any less animalistic in our primal needs
and desires.

We often forget that the label of 'human' is just a classification
in the animal kingdom, and that we share the same basic instincts
and biology as all other living creatures."

The more we try to distance ourselves from our animal nature,
the more we lose touch with the very essence of what it means
to be alive.

Humans may have built empires and invented technology, but
we are still animals at heart, subject to the same laws of nature as
the rest of the living world

Artificial intelligence, What is the relevance?

We are the most dangerous creature

Humans, animals, one in the same Nature's creations, with different
names Both with instincts that drive the game To hunt and gather, to
survive and claim

But humans, with intelligence and grace Have the power to change

their fate To rise above their primal base And create a world that's truly great
Yet still we struggle with our beast The urge to take and to consume To dominate and to feast On resources, as if our own room
But let us remember, we are part Of the natural world, not apart Let us live in harmony, with heart And preserve what we call art
For in the end, we are but a link In the chain of life, that never sinks Let us strive to make our mark And leave a legacy, not just a spark.

• **Smile**

Smiles are like sunshine, Bringing warmth to the heart, A simple curve of the lips, Can make a brand new start.
With a smile on our face, The world seems a brighter place, It can chase away the gloom, And light up a room.
A smile is contagious, It's easy to share, One smile can start a chain reaction, Of joy everywhere.
So let's wear a smile, With pride on our face, For in this world of troubles, It's a small act of grace.
With a smile we can show, That we're happy to be here, With a smile we can make, Someone's day a little more dear.
So let us smile often, And let it shine bright, For a world filled with smiles, Is a world that's just right.
Smile, never give up, That is not us

For now, here is a smile, Grace, style, Even if something goes wrong I can run a mile

I forgot what I was mad about, Smile from your heart to your mouth

• **Deep end**

Deep waters, dark and mysterious A realm of secrets yet to be revealed The depth holds creatures most ferocious And treasures that have yet to be sealed

The ocean floor, a world unknown A place of silence, void of sound Where the weight of the water is shown And the pressure pushes down

But in the depths, there is beauty A wonderland of coral and reef A symphony of color and duty A natural masterpiece

Deep waters, a mystery to explore A place of danger, yet to be adored A world of wonder, forevermore A deep sea treasure to be stored.

Prideful get a wide view, swim, Be fearless of the unknown, Echoes from the noise

New heights soaring, Rather be ridiculous than boring Narratives, views, different particles, Fairy tales, Imagine dragons, They can be conquered too

Still is the water, The creatures below are different, Sun shines on all Alone in the deep end can't quit

Deep waters, dark and cold, Mysteries yet to unfold, Secrets hidden in the deep, Where none but the bravest dare to leap.

The ocean's depths are a vast unknown, A world of creatures yet to be shown, A place of beauty and of fear, Where danger lurks with every peer.

But still we dive, with hearts of fire, To explore the depths, to quell desire, To see what lies beneath the waves, And unlock the ocean's deepest caves.

So let us brave the deep waters, And find what lies within, For in the depths, our hearts will soar, And we will find true beauty again.

Regardless of the margin, Stay in the deep end

• **Hell's Utopia**

Deep in the fiery pits below Where souls in torment come and go A place of eternal suffering Where the damned are forever writhing

The flames of hell are ever burning A constant fire, never turning

The screams of the damned echo loud In this eternal, fiery shroud

No mercy in this place of woe No respite from the pain to know

Eternally damned and forsaken In this fiery, eternal maw

But let this be a warning true To all who would do wicked deeds For in the end, in hell you'll dwell And eternal fire is all you'll need

Sin City has nothing on me, Electricity before New York City, Give a heckler a koch, Paint your house Bansky, Hanky Panky

Entertainment hand in hand with arraignment, Everything is drug, Indulge, War with us, Spartacus, Monopoly, chance, ticket , Sell their soul for a biscuit.

Grudges not held, facts remembered, Ax not buried but in arm's reach, For the judgemental, Til the judge fucks with their mental

For the birds, Peck at it, petty tricks

Easier to clean dirt than blood, Why is the devil the one they love?

All of the above

• Munchin on fur

Juicy and plump, a fruit so sweet,In my hands, it begs to be eaten
I take a bite, the flavors burst, My senses are awakened, my thirst
Greedily,
I devour the fruit whole, With each bite, my hunger takes control
The sweet nectar drips down my chin, As I relish in the taste of sin
I cannot stop, I must have more, The fruit is my addiction, my never-
ending score
I feast until there's nothing left, But a pit and a seed, a fruit bereft
Sated and content, I lay back and sigh
The fruit was my pleasure, my guilty high,But the taste still lingers on
my tongue
A reminder of my fruit-filled binge, unendingly young
Body Electric, Trying to put those blocks together like Tetris,
What does the weather do? Raining cats and dogs, eating that cat like
a dog
let me devour you, GRRR, Muchin on fur

• **Diss-Missed**

Ignore the words that sting and hurt, Let them pass like clouds in the sky. For they are but the ramblings of a mind, Full of anger and malice, not worth your time.

Do not let their insults define you, For you are so much more than they see. You are strong, you are brave, And their words can never take that away.

Stand tall and proud, Let their insults slide off your back. For in the end, it is they who will be consumed, By the hatred they have chosen to stack.

So ignore the insults, let them be, For they are but a whisper on the wind. You are greater than any word they say, And your light will always shine within.

The butt of a joke or an assault, Too many rats will never dig a good hole

Dissing will never get old, No fucks given, If I am shitted on by a pigeon

Am I to be offended by what you say, Sure the pen is mightier than the sword

Words cut deep, Unbothered to say the least

It must take up a lot of space in your head, Any response will go over your head

Take the higher road, Gift for Christmas, their diss missed

• Listened but didn't hear

A poor listener, so quick to speak, Thoughts they share without a peek, Of what their ears might have to say, To listen's not their chosen way.

They talk and talk, with nary a break, For the thoughts they share, they can't wait, To let you speak, to share your mind

Poor listeners, with ears so deaf, They hear not words, but only half, They nod and smile, but understand, Not a thing, in the speaker's hand.

They're quick to judge, and slow to hear, They interrupt, and make it clear, That they're not interested, in what's said, But only in, their own voice in their head.

Poor listeners, with minds so closed, They miss the gems, that would have disclosed, The beauty of a different view, The wisdom of a different hue.

So let us be, good listeners true, With open hearts, and minds anew, And hear the words, that others speak, And let them guide, our hearts and feet.

• Church

Don't insult my intelligence, you speak no relevance
greed's the only snake that can't be tamed
Preaching to the masses, With words that ring so true,
Guiding them to righteousness, And helping them break through.
With tales of hope and glory, And stories of the past,
Spread the word, And make our message last.
We speak of sin and redemption, Of love that knows no bounds,
We urge the lost to find salvation, And turn their hearts around.
We stand before the crowd, And raise our voices high,
Preaching to the people, With the strength of the sky.
For in the word of God, There is a truth that's pure,
And through our preaching, He will always endure.
Not that heavy, cheap shot's got me feeling like HOT already,
How I feel about your peace and harmony AKANELE
What's good for the goose is good for the gander,
Got answers, Banter, Slander

• **JOB**

I do not mind climbing the corporate ladder
But if it's for peanuts I am not playing snakes and ladders
Jobs, jobs, everywhere, In offices, factories, and the street. Each one a
chance to prove and share Our skills, our talents, our fleet.
From the builder to the banker, The nurse to the teacher, Each job
plays a vital role, In shaping our world, our future.
Some jobs are grand and some are small, But all are important, that is
true. For in each one, we give our all, And make a difference, anew.
Jobs may be hard, or they may be fun, But all are necessary, it's true.
For each one helps us on the run, Of life, and all it's due.
So let us cherish every role, In the jobs that we pursue, For they shape
our heart, our soul, And make our lives anew.
Capital gains remedies dignity, The typical job won't afford you
opulence
so transverse where the river is depthless
Wealth and unconditional happiness is an oxymorons,
hunting two hens won't get you any
Appetite for fish, stomach for beans ,The deed is just a seed, water it,
prune it, recipe to succeed
Jobs we do, big and small, Each one unique, standing tall. From the
builder to the baker, Each one a vital part, a maker.
The teacher educates the youth, The farmer grows the food, in truth.
The doctor cures the sick and ill, The artist's work, a beauty still.
The tech worker codes with care, The musician fills the air. The
writer pens a story true, The scientist, a discovery new.
All these jobs, and many more, Each one, an important chore. For
without them, where would we be? Lost and directionless, you see.
So let us appreciate and cheer, For all the jobs, far and near. For each
one, plays a role, In making our world whole.

SHE/HER

What vexes men? HER

Wild and free, untamable women With fire in their eyes and wind in their hair Their strength and spirit cannot be broken Their hearts beat with a passion rare

They march to the beat of their own drum And blaze their own trail They are warriors, fierce and strong, And cannot be thrown in jail

They stand tall, unafraid In the face of hate and fear For they know their worth And will not shed a tear

Untamable women, a force to be reckoned Their power undeniable, their spirit unbroken They are the queens of their own destiny And nothing can stop them, not even tyranny

So let them roam, let them fly For they are the ones who will change the world With their fierce determination And their untamed, unfurled

So here's to the wild and free, The untamable women of today May their light continue to shine And light the way

Gentlemen allow her to maintain her fiction, Avocado is not a vegetable, naturally a rebel

form of a mesomorph, heart of Sirsee Lannister, her satisfaction and men's destruction

Great form all the tricks, just know she's salt like potato chips

Stolen time, this dime appraised a penny

untamed and true, Women of spirit, fierce and new, With fire in their eyes and grace in their step, They walk the earth, a force to be kept.

Their hearts are pure, their souls unbroken, Their will unshakable, their words unspoken, They rise above the fray, unafraid to fight, For what they believe, for what is right.

They are the wind that blows through the trees, The waves that crash upon the seas, The sun that rises every morn, The light that guides us through the storm.

For they are untamable, these women of power, With their heads held high, they tower, Above the rest, they pave their way, For all to see, for all to say.

So let us honor these women of strength, For their beauty and grace, for their will, no length, Will ever tame their hearts and minds, For they are untamable, of this we are reminded.

evolved destiny, lost friends and money for the devil next to me
Her aggregate's equivalent inconsequential
She's repugnant and foul, clear to identify like a vowel

- **Friends like THESE**

Bad friends, like poison in the cup, Stealing joy and causing rough, With words like knives they cut and sting, Leaving wounds that hurt and cling.

They talk behind your back with glee, And spread their lies so all can see, They take and take without a care, And leave you feeling lost and scared.

But true friends, like a shining light, Bring warmth and joy to darkest night, With words of kindness, they lift you high, And make your troubles disappear and fly.

So let the bad friends go their way, And choose true friends to light your way, For in this life, it's friends we need, To help us through each trial and deed.

On the table sugar and salt look the same unlabeled, Tell a fictional tale of misfortune, see the grin. Friends at times, are enemies guised, but defense from the enemy is a given from a friend it is difficult, sooner or later you realize,Expected and forgiven

As I'd like my transgressions to be,I forgive you,

The statement holds true, With friends like these who needs enemies

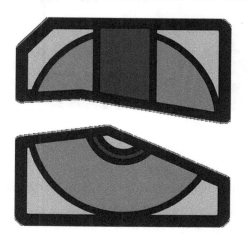

• My perfect IMPERFECTION

A blemish on the skin, a curve in the nose, A freckle on the cheek, a quirk in the toes. A stutter in the speech, a stumble in the walk, These imperfections make us unique, they are the mark.

We strive for perfection, but it's an illusion, For perfection is dull, it's a lack of fusion. It's the imperfections that make us alive, That give our existence depth and drive.

So embrace your imperfections, let them shine, For they make you who you are, they make you divine. Perfection is overrated, it's just a show, But the beauty of the imperfection, that's where the real glow.

So let your quirks and flaws be known, For it's the imperfections that

make you unique and grown. The perfect imperfection, that's what we
are, So celebrate and love it, it's your unique star.
Perception,half of what we hear and none of what we see,
Eyes are the window to the soul, Is everything that we perceive it all
to be?
Thoughts perceived or far-fetched? Hard to believe
100 people won't wait for one, The show must go on

• **Talk that talk**

Speak confidently, let your words take flight, With grace and poise, let
your voice be bright
Do not falter, do not cower in fear, For your voice is strong, it is
music to the ear
Stand tall and proud, with your head held high, Your message is
important, let it reach the sky
Do not doubt yourself, or your power to speak, For your words are
valuable, they are unique
Speak confidently, let your words be heard, For they will inspire, they
will empower, they will stir
Do not let others silence your voice, For you have a story, a choice
So speak confidently, let your words shine,For you are the speaker,
and you are divine.
trash or treasure, judged by endeavors,
clever fools who are clairvoyant but can never see the truth

Every vegetable has its time,but we disregard time, neglect the beauty
in all things seen or unseen, Don't jump above your head
Hunger, chance while the clear opportunity to take will tempt the
most righteous
hungry belly does not have ears, The tongue's weightless yet only a
few can subsist it
Running their mouth the only exercise, jumping to conclusions or
talking in circles,
Words mightier than the sword, strength by your spirit, underhanded
hear, cheer it
use it for fuel as a tool,You are the jewel, Talk that talk

• Mikan under the kotasu

Beneath the warmth of heated table, Sitting with my tangerine,
Peeling back the rind so fine, Juice drips down my chin like wine.
The sun is shining through the glass, As I enjoy my citrus repast, The
tangy flavor, oh so bright, Fills my senses with pure delight.
The world outside is cold and gray, But under here, I'm here to stay,
With my tangerine, my simple treat, I am complete, so warm and sweet.
So let the snow and winds outside, Rage on, with all their might, For
I am here, with my dear fruit, Beneath the warmth, in my own pursuit.
Pensive is the mood, Relaxation gratifies us
sitting under a heated table eating a tangerine is euphoric

• **I thought to myself**

Deep in my mind, thoughts swirl and collide, A jumbled mess that I cannot hide.

An endless stream of doubts and fears, That I hold close and never clear.

Memories of past mistakes and woes, Echo through my mind like ghostly foes.

But amidst the chaos and the pain, There lies a spark, a hope to gain.

For within the depths of my soul, There lies a strength that makes me whole.

I'll face my fears and doubts head on, And find a way to push beyond.

For deep in my mind, there's a light, That guides me through the darkest night.

And though my thoughts may be confused, I'll find the strength to be renewed.

Inner thoughts, a mystery untold Whispers in the mind, stories yet to be told A labyrinth of emotions, deep and wide A journey within, to one's own self to abide

Memories, dreams, and fears all in play A symphony of thoughts, in the mind all day A cacophony at times, overwhelming the soul A burden to bear, that can make one feel old

But in this chaos, lies a hidden gem A light in the darkness, a guide to the end A voice of reason, a beacon of hope A way to navigate, this mind's endless scope

• **Model Role**

Good role models are like shining stars, Guiding us through life's darkest hours. With wisdom and grace they show us the way, Teaching us to be kind and strong each day.

Bad role models, on the other hand, Bring us down and lead us to despair. They show us the wrong path, and make us stray, Teaching us to be bitter and to tear.

But in the end, it's our choice to make, To follow the good or to make the same mistake. Let us choose wisely, let us not be swayed, For the path we choose will shape our fate.

So let us look to the shining stars, And let them guide us through life's harshest wars. For with their light, we'll find our way, To a brighter tomorrow, and a future that's sure.

• **Ramble**

Words flow like a river, Endless and wild, Thoughts tumbling, Mindless rambling piled.

Ideas swirling, Like leaves in a storm, No direction, Just a chaotic
form.
A jumbled mess, Of thoughts and ideas, No rhyme or reason, Just a
stream of tears.
But in the chaos, Beauty can be found, A glimpse of truth, In the
rambling sound.
So let the words flow, And the mind ramble on, For in the flow,
Wisdom can be drawn.

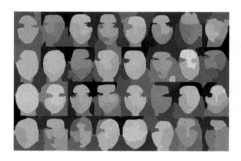

• **How I feel vs. How I look**

Are people really happy, or do they just pretend? A facade of smiles,
to hide the pain within.
They laugh and joke, and say they're fine, But deep down, are they
truly happy, or just resigned?
They hide behind their screens and social feeds, Posting pictures of
their perfect lives, but do they really believe?
The world is full of pain and sorrow, And sometimes it feels like
there's no tomorrow.
But true happiness lies in the things we can't see, In the love we share
and the memories.
So let us be real, and let our hearts be true, And maybe, just maybe,
we'll find happiness too.

- **Temper Temper**

Temper flares like a fiery sun, A force to be reckoned with. It rises quickly, one by one, And leaves destruction in its path.
It's a tempest in a teapot, A storm in a small space. It's a dragon that won't be caught, A fire that can't be tamed or chased.
But though it may be fierce and wild, Temper can be controlled. It's a choice to let it rage and build, Or to keep it in check, and hold.
For when we master our own temper, We can weather any storm. We can rise above the flames and ember, And find peace where once was warm.
So let us not let temper rule, But choose to be the masters of our fate. For when we control our own tempest, We'll find serenity, not hate.
Temper, Temper,I said I regret darn you, Robbed me of my peace
Bike without brakes, A car without a steering, Lost control, From the jeering
I bottled it up, Poised, relaxed, Unexpectedly it erupted,
Like a volcano,
Momentary Insanity, No brain yo, Then snap
What can I remember, Temper Temper

- **Forces**

Bombs fall like rain from the sky Screams fill the air, a haunting cry
Buildings crumble, cities in ruin Death and destruction, a never-ending
ruin
Soldiers march, with heads held high Fighting for a cause, they know
not why Brothers in arms, united as one But in the end, what have they
won?
Families torn apart, children without a home Lives lost, forever to
roam War, a cruel and bitter game Leaving nothing but sorrow and
shame
But amidst the chaos and the pain There are those who choose to
remain With hope in their hearts and love in their eyes They will rebuild
and rise
For though war may take its toll It is the human spirit that makes us
whole And though we may falter and we may fall We will always stand
tall.

• **Realize**

Conquer's heart trumps the arrogance of a king
Enlightenment comes like a dawn Bringing new light to what was
once gone A lifting of the veil, a shift in sight A newfound understand-
ing, all is bright
It brings a peace that surpasses all A calm that answers the mind's call
The world is seen in a different hue No longer clouded by what we knew
The path to enlightenment is long But the journey makes us strong

With every step, we learn and grow And the beauty of the world we
know
So let us strive to reach that height Where all is clear, and all is right
For in enlightenment, we find our way And see the beauty of each new
day

Printed in the USA
CPSIA information can be obtained
at www.ICGtesting.com
LVHW062238060823
754499LV00010B/286